Jessica Lucci

# Freedom for Me

Copyright 2018 by Jessica Lucci and Indie Woods

All rights reserved.

No part of this publication may be reproduced, stored in a retrieval system, or transmitted, in any form or by any means, electronic, mechanical, photocopying, recording, or otherwise, without written permission of the author.

Cover photo and author photo by Linda Utley Harrington.

www.JessicaLucci.org

www.IndieWoods.org

Printed in the United States of America

# Dedication

With love to my best friend who saved my life.  11:11

# Author's Note

Domestic violence takes many forms. They are all ugly. It is not your fault. You are not alone. People care, and value you. Bless them by allowing them to bless you. It's your turn to be helped. It's your time to be free.

# Freedom For Me

# An Ally

    The Warrior pulls her heavy shield through the mud

    As her armor sags on the ground

    Leaving spiral tracks tinged with blood

    Where green grass might have been found

    Dragging her splintered feet through the night

    Sleeping with brief dreams of a new day

    Darkness erasing her bright sight

    While any light left flickers away


    A voice echoes across the gravelly sky

    Like thunder with no lightening

    A growl of a wolf prowling nearby

Low and faint but not frightening

Unhesitant yet bewildered

The Warrior listens to the gruff message

Imagining a promise delivered

Freedom without carnage

# Another Day

I know I could cry

But not right now

Not today

# Another Moon

Youth has passed me by

Like a hopeless dream

In the day I cling to

The love of a lie

At night I still scream

In my head to be true

# Another Year

All that I hear is the sound

The sound

The sound of another year

Smash

To the ground

All that I hear is the sound

The sound

The sound of another year

Smash

To the ground

All that I see is the sight

The sight

The sight of another year
Flash
To the light
All that I see is the sight
The sight
The sight of another year
Flash
To the light

All that I feel is the breath
The breath
The breath of another year
Crash
To our death
All that I feel is the breath
The breath
The breath of another year

Crash

To our death

# A Piece of Hope

Looking for a piece of hope

One fragmented shard

To pierce through my veins

Wisdom, patience, does me no good

# Around

<u>Around me the sound</u>

The sound of another year

Smashing to the ground

# Apple

    I have two drinks

    and I hear these sappy songs

    and I cry to myself

    and I suck it up

    and I ask myself

    What the FUCK is wrong with me?

    I've WORKED too FUCKIN much

    I've TRIED too FUCKIN hard

Hiding my face
from myself
I quickly wipe the tears away

I remember the vows I have made
    but in the darkness
      in the back of my brain
I wonder

what honour is there in that

I want to do what's right
I will steal and rob
      but only if it's necessary
I would kill the person
      who could ever hurt my child
but only after
decades of torturing them


Can I admit
that what I feel
Is not
a game
to myself?

I am not trying
to escape
anything
I'd like to think
I'm stronger than that

I am cursed
by my conscience

I don't want to hurt anyone
Is this the devil I am listening to?
Because the thoughts I hear
    make SO much sense
    but somewhere
    deep inside
I KNOW
something is not right

Is it okay
    to ignore
    the facts?
Is it alright
    to let
    love rule?
Do I hear Satan
    calling again
If God is Love
    how can Love be Bad?

# Bare

Bare branches crying icicles

Frozen in limbo

Timeless

Futureless

Christmasless

# Bitter

     Thank you God for giving me a hint of anger

     When I was expressing my concern over moving too fast too soon with increased visitation, he said

BOO HOO

And I rose up and was not afraid

I turned to him and said,

NO! That is a mean thing to say! That is HURTFUL! Don't say that to me

I could have never said that a year ago

NEVER AGAIN

# Captured

The warrior lays down her sword

If she gives up the battle

She is not defeated

If she surrenders

She hasn't lost

# Crying in my Sweat

Music pounding through my veins

the rhythm in my head

I work my body hard enough

to feel the rush instead

of the pain lingering in my soul

My muscles beat me down to the bones

Til the tears on my face mix with the sweat

and I don't remember why I'm wet


Is my flesh on fire

with passion's desire

When I fall to the floor will I find

that my body is here but I've lost my mind

The lyrics hit me in the chest and I can't breathe

The words pound in my heart and I can't believe

All the suffering I endured, so much pain

I have lost so much, what did I gain

Could I have stopped it then

all time begins with a question

Why did I let who do what and when

If only someone had slapped some sense into me

would I have opened my eyes, would I see

The trouble that my life was in

How could I not know what was going to begin

Now I am in a world of my own

my own doubt, my own debt, my own misery

But the anchors holding onto me

are the lives which I also am trying to free

I clutch at my knees

my hair in my face

I am disgusted

with my sad embrace

and the tears start to fall

as I sit on the floor

and cry out to no one

no more, no more

# Cut

one shard

of my broken glass heart

might still care

and I am afraid

that one sliver

will pierce through

what is left of my strength

and make all my blood flow out

# Days and Nights

 Y'know, I can't remember the last time he held and kissed me

 But he tries to feel me up every night

 He can go the whole day without talking to me

 Can walk by without looking me in my eyes

 And I scream inside

 Don't you see me

 Why does he only find me

 when it is dark and cold

 In the daytime I shudder

 How can I be so alone

Every morning I make his coffee for him

And every day I get our kids ready for school

I prepare him food every afternoon

And every evening I cook dinner


But I sit at the table

And feel like starving

I can't bear to bring food to my lips

When I look at my children I force food into my mouth

And have two drinks


At night I stay up as late as I can

I work, I clean,

I prepare for the next day

I lay down on the couch

and a movie keeps me company

Because I am hiding from

the company he keeps

Stealthily I climb up the stairway

I kiss my sleeping children in their beds

And sometimes I crawl in next to them

Other times I choose my own bed

When it is very very very late at night

And I am so tired from waiting

And I hope to sleep

Without being stripped

And all night is a tug o war

With my clothes

And my desire

And my dignity might break like a rope tied around my neck

# Deafening

Soundless in a thunderclap

A bolt of lightening on my lap

Stunning, stirring,

Disbelieving

Momentary brightness

Pain endless

# Destructive Tears

I can't cry over

What might have been

Anymore

What if

If only

Going back in time

Not today

# Disgust and Desire

My disgust

is greater

than my desire

Closing my eyes

seeing a blank face

A nobody

A stranger

To replace who I am really with

Keeping my mind separate

from my body

I don't know how I do it

But I do it

All the time

Crying

Numbness

If I imagine someone
who I actually yearn for
my spirit crashes against the wall
of my grasped body
and screams out silently
to stop

No more
I am ending this game
For the sake of sanity
For the sake of moving on
For the sake of a tiny fragment of dignity

For the sake of what my heart throbs for

# Don't Say I'm Stoic

Don't tell me not to be tough
Don't say to show my pain
I am barely brave enough
To not weep in endless rain

It takes every fiber of my being
To be strong within these walls
Maybe I won't stop crying
If one teardrop falls

I clench my teeth together
And bite the grief beneath
Maybe the tears will flow forever
If I lose one breath of strength

# Dragon Slayer

Have you ever watched

a dragon die

Choking to death

on its own smoky breath

I don't want to slay this beast

Not because I am afraid

I can't bear to drive a sword

into its pathetic heart

But as I watch its eyes roll back

and see the blood drip from its mouth

I curse it and wish it would

just hurry up and die

I have been eaten alive
Burned through my soul
Claws clutching my life

Breathing the noxious fumes
The taste of death in my mouth
Venom on my lips

I kick and prod it
Taunt it
Tempt it towards death
or to take one last bite
and kill me at last

# Eclipse

I sit in warm sun

Under a blue cloudless sky

Why didn't Job die

# Endless Climb

The Warrior gave up the crawl
Weapons ready but never drawn
Evasive battles never won
Never even fought at all

Slowly climbing one more hill
Gripping onto nothing still
No end in sight
Just more pain
No truth in what might
Be poison rain

When will all the torture cease

When will she find true release

When will she awake to the day

When justice has finally found her way

# Existence

I am an invisible mirror

Unseen until the light hits

Shining reflecting

Off blankness

# Figured Out

He finally figured out that I am human

He finally figured out that I know I'm not perfect

He finally figured out that I need attention

He finally figured out that he is not the sun, he is not the one


But I would've

But I still would've


I would've still stayed with him

I would've done my best by him

I would've given all my life

I would've been the best wife

There is so little that I need
And he gave me so little

How our stories are so different
amazes me
His version of our life together
contradicts my own
But I sat and listened
Calm, and kind
I didn't fight
I asked him, why should I?

Why should I fight?
Why should I cry?
Argue all night
To hold onto a lie?

I don't want to convince him

to care about me

Either he does or he doesn't, that's not for me to create

I will accept my fate

# Flight

Where will I go?

What will I do?

What will I see?

Who will I know?

How can I go on

in a world I don't even know?

I have been living in these walls

for so long I can't imagine what it's like outside

Nobody else will know

how to talk to me

Nobody else will know

that I have been living here like this
How will I look them in the eyes?
How will I go on with my days?
I don't even know
where I am supposed to sleep at night

Why can't we run away?
I would love to take the children
on an adventure around the world
Someone else must know who we are
Someone else must feel our pain
Someone else must know our desire
to enjoy the world in a peaceful life

Where do I go
How can I stay
Why can't I live

with my children in a happy home, us together?

# For the World to See

    I am not invisible anymore

    No longer a ghost drifting through the door

    I am seen through the lies

    People look in my eyes

    I have lived through the death of a false love that cries


    Not everyone can see me now

    It is still not safe everywhere somehow

    There is a part of me I need to hide

    A thrill in my heart remains locked inside

    Which in time will burst forth to the earth open wide

I still need to be free

For the world to see

# Freedom

Freedom

is knowing

I will never let him touch me again

like that

and if he does try,

I will fight him

I will struggle

I will leave a mark

so the world will know

that I am not willing

to be his toy

anymore

# Frozen

Frozen in limbo

Branches crying icicles

Timeless; Christmasless

# Game Over

The winner takes it all
And I hate to lose
But this time I'll fall
If I get to choose

I will stop this game
I don't want to play
It will never be the same
It went on too long anyway

I played by the rules
I moved fair
Now I'm the one who's
Going to dare

I don't want to win
I don't want control
Keeping things going
Has taken its toll

Leave the cards where they lay
Fold up the board
Place the pieces away
Don't try another word

I don't want to play anymore
Blame me for the forfeit
I've been a sore loser before
But this is the end of it

# Good Night

I don't like being the only one awake

I used to like this time alone

But lately

It only reminds me

Of how alone I am

This time of night

Every song makes me cry

And I don't want to know why

I don't want to know

I really don't mind

Being alone

But lonely

Is another thing

And maybe I drink too much
Watching the clock
Waiting for the world to fall asleep
So I can creep into bed

But then my thoughts still curse me
And I have to block them out
Either give in
Or give out

The night
Gives me no cover
The darkness
Is no shelter
Now that the truth is clear to me

This isn't the life I want to live

So I'll drink more
Until I don't understand myself
Because that's better
Than admitting the truth

The time I've wasted
The hope I've failed
The strength I've faked
The love I've missed out on

And so now
I'm surrounded by "friends"
Who probably
Delight in talking crap about me
But I could care less

Sure, I'd like to be liked

But at what expense

If I can't be myself

I can't be somebody else

# Grapes of Wrath

How can she eat the grapes of wrath

Taste that bitter wine

Of fresh fruit still on the vine

When her children are still on the borderline


How can she breathe in the aftermath

Feel the soft sunshine

With fingers intertwined

When her children haven't crossed that line


How can she close her eyes

With each tender kiss

Knowing the life she will never miss
How can she give in to this

When her flesh and blood are still at war
The way it was threatened before
She can't be free as she falls to the floor
She can't take it anymore

# Handstands

I don't want you to catch me

How dare you offer

I want to fall

I'll take the bruises

I'd rather crumple to the floor

Than have you help me

You are incompetent

You will drop me anyway

Maybe that is your plan

I can't even begin to figure out

Why you don't leave me alone

Yet force me into isolation

I will hit the ground a thousand times

And the pain will invigorate me

Because it is my will, my ambition

I am giving everything I can

Even when it hurts me

I can take the crash if I can only

Plummet away from you

And land broken

But alive

Never to be thrown

Never to be pushed down

My body and my mind

Aches to escape your touch and control

# Heartless

I am the one

who used to love

and gave every effort

to belief

I was the one

who took a chance

and held on

for dear life


I am the one

who used to hope

and gave my heart and soul

to faith

I was the one

who tried again

and forgave

anything

I am the one

who used to trust

and gave all honesty

to this life

I was the one

who never lied

and told the truth

all the time

I am the one

who used to care

and gave my mind and body

to that dead end

I was the one

who gave it all

whatever I could

no matter what

I am the one

who doesn't love

who doesn't hope

who doesn't trust

who doesn't care

I am the one

who won't take that chance

who won't try again

who won't stop the lie

who won't give it all

Not again

Not anymore

I have finally learned

And I have chosen

I am heartless

# He Doesn't Look At Me Like That

Music videos in the morning

I do crunches on the floor

He steps over me

To his cereal

Listening to jazz

I slowly twist my hips

He stares at the computer

Turned away from me

But if he notices someone look at me

Or if I mention something funny, unthinking

About a guy smiling at me,

He gets mad at me

I have finally learned

To keep my mouth shut

And not joke around

And close my eyes to the world

That he doesn't want me to see


Hours drizzle on

Sitting on the couch

The cold space of inches between us

Makes my soul shiver

As somewhere in the frozen chamber of my heart

Blood pours out

Crackling with the desire

To be touched and warmed

Silence

Walking right by me

Do I exist?

It is maddening

When the absence of the day

Changes to the prodding of the night

And all the physical touch I craved since I awoke

Is thrust upon me in my tiredness

Those brief moments

He tries to

Be "sweet"

Or "thoughtful"

Seem like funhouse mirrors

Where the image is skewed
And it is hard for me to see
Clearly

It is so strange
To be stalked
By the person
Living with me

The up and down
Rollercoaster
I can't take it anymore
I am not riding it now
But I am watching it like a movie
So even though
It isn't really happening to me
I still feel it

In an outsiders view

Seeing my life
From the outside
For the first time
Is shocking
And sad
And confusing

# He Knows

He knows who I am now

Now he knows

Now he's fucked

# Holding Darkness

She doesn't hold darkness
But darkness holds her
Without fairness
Every hour

Yet the light shines down
Even in the deep night
It still goes on
Showing what is right

Sometimes she can't see
And can't find her way
Will she ever feel free
Maybe someday

# Holding My Hand

In the dark shadow

of a dead tree

I stand alone

holding my hands out to the sun

and I feel warmth

from a friend

# Honour

He walked out the door

to bring me something

and I said, no, no, no, please no

And while I waited for the door to open again

I fell to my knees

and cried

And all the things I begged of God,

forgiveness, mercy, and relief,

I do not know what I'll be blessed with

but I will accept what comes

And then he returned,

and the words he said to me

as he edged closer on the couch

froze my heart

and made me want to die

made me want to erase my life

He said

God wants us to honor each other

and anyway

isn't that what we promised to do

But all of the words that he's ever said

echo in my numb mind

All the accusations

the cynicism

the little stinging remarks I laugh off

the questions I won't answer

the insults

the soundless sneer

I think I remember

he used to say

he loved me

and I believed

I think a long time ago

he used to write me love songs

and leave flowers by the door

And I know the times I pleaded

please, I don't need much, but here's what I need

and how he'd dismiss my tears

or try for a day

and then I would be alone in my heart again

And honour

Yes, I can honour

And I have honoured

Always

And I know I have sinned

I have stopped honouring,

because I just feel

there is nothing to honour anymore

# Hot Tub

Burn his fingerprints

From my skin

Boil his scent

From my body

Scrape his touch

From my flesh

No water can be hot enough

Fingernails aren't sharp enough

To cut through layers of nerves

To erase him from my being

My arms are red and raw

My face is flushed and feverish

I almost feel faint

Immersed in steam

# I Did

I could have lit a match

to rebuild the flame

I could have danced so sexy

to bring the groove back

I could have read and learned

to grow and become more interesting

I could have given everything

anytime

anywhere

I could have done so much, and I did

I did

I did

The fire wasn't burning out

the smoke was choking me in my sleep

The music was so loud

all I heard was muffled noise in my pillow at night

My books, I was illiterate

in a still, empty airless library of blank cutting pages

I gave everything

every time

every where

I did so much, I did

I did

I did

# I Don't Care

Forgive me, Father,

for the worst sin of all

Forgive me, Father

for not being sorry

I don't feel sorry at all


And I don't care

I don't care

that what I want is wrong

I don't care

I just don't care

I want this sin

It's what I've wanted all along

Forgive me, Father

and listen, please

You know what I've been through

So numb on my knees

Don't I deserve this?

Can't I get a break?

When do I get my chance?

What else must I take?


And I don't care

I don't care

And I don't want to hear

how what I want is wrong

I don't care

I just don't care

I've been waiting for so long

When is it my turn?

What lesson must I learn?

I'm tired of being good.

always doing what I should

I've been a good mother,

and I will be forever

Been a patient wife

But I want this sin in my life

# I Don't Know What To Do

I thought I was strong, that's what people tell me anyway.

If I am so strong, could I be resilient?

Maybe I could just go on, live through this, and give up.

I don't need to win.

I don't even think I feel the need to do the "right" thing anymore.

I am just so tired, and I am afraid that I have finally been worn down.

I don't know what to do next.

Can I really do this, wouldn't it be completely awful of me if I actually LEFT with the children?

Wouldn't that be a terrible thing to do?

Maybe it would be better if I just said, okay, I give up, whatever you say... and agree to everything.

Agree that I am an angry person who doesn't care the way a normal human being does.

Agree that I am full of anger and hate.

Agree that I am mean.

Agree to all the lies.

And at night, just take sleeping pills and close my eyes and not struggle.

I think I am ready for that.

I think I could do that.

# I Don't Remember

I don't remember

my name anymore

but I know who I am

Hidden forever

boundless troubadour

former lives

forged from buckram

# If

It is good you don't know

What I go through

Because if you knew

You would cry for me

And I don't want

Any of that pity

But if it was you

I'd cry for you

# If I Needed A Friend

If I showed up at your door
what would you do?

If you saw tears hidden in my eyes
what would you say?

If I had nowhere to go
Would you take me in?

If I couldn't talk
Would you listen to my silent cry?

If I sat here

alone and afraid

Would you let me know

That you see my words

and remind me

that I exist


Would you protect my children for me?

Would you serve them a meal?

Would you smile at them and play a game with them,

bring them some brief happiness?


If I had to go

would you cover for me?


If I knew you wouldn't understand

would you accept me anyway?

If you saw me walking on the sidewalk
would you wave
to let me know
that you recognize me
and I am not invisible?

If I needed money for a cab
would you hand me cash
without ever asking for it back

If I needed to pack in a hurry
would you come over with boxes
and a screwdriver
so I could bring my curtains with me?

If what you saw in my life

didn't make sense to you

would you take my word for it

and believe me?

# If You Could Tell Me

If you could tell me what to be

I could be it

If you could tell me how to act

I could act it

I could be on my best behavior

Calm and polite,

Sipping daintily,

Without a hint of bite

Quiet now the children

Peaceful in their way

Dreamy little children

Doing as I say
In their own way

I could be
What you want me to be
Not for you
Just direct me

If I only knew what you wanted from me
I could be it
Because I have it

I am dreamy
I am mild
I am easy
Like a child
I am thoughtful

I am bold

I am careful

If I'm told


I'm the prophet

I can tell you what is true

If you believe it

I could believe in you

# I Know He'll Find Me

In the parking lot

The motor still running

Sitting

Trying to breathe

Shame and grief

Bleed from fear

I am working up the courage

To walk into the grocery store

What if he is in there?

Sometimes the world goes white

When I see his mirage

What is wrong with me

I am mad at myself for feeling this way

Will I always be this way

All my power to not cry

# I'm Still Alive

I'm still alive

I fight the good fight

Escaping the darkness

Bewildered by the light

I'm still alive

My breath is my own

Away from the blankness

Amazed by my sight

I'm still alive

# Independence

I don't need vengeance

I don't even need justice

I do need freedom

# Independence Day

No one knew the storm I'd been through

As I smiled through the pain of sharp rain

I pretended it was fine, getting better all the time

But the truth was making me feel insane

The kids were only 6 and 9 that summer

And I am glad that there's a lot they forget

But one thing I hope they'll always remember

Is the peace we had never known yet

Nobody knew, nobody saw

The signs were hidden and deep

But slowly I heard the cries so raw

Screaming from my dreams in my sleep


Well, people whisper, and people talk

Sometimes their hearts don't meet their heads

But I was lucky to walk the lonely walk

Holding the hands of a few true friends


I know I'm free, forever free

I want the world to know there is life after misery

If I'm weak or strong, if I'm right or wrong

I will not regret, I have left that threat, it's Independence Day

Every day, it's Independence Day

I needed a friend when I reached the end

I packed up fast and I ran and I hid

It took the worst crime to make up my mind

It's the bravest thing I ever did


Sometimes I wonder if I did the right thing

If I could've kept going on

But in my heart freedom sings

Through my weakness I became strong


I know I'm free, forever free

I want the world to know there is life after misery

If I'm weak or strong, if I'm right or wrong

I will not regret, I have left that threat, it's Independence Day

Every day, it's Independence Day

The more that's been taken away

The more which I have had to leave

It only makes me more free every day

And gives me more reason to believe

Sometimes I still wonder and I still cry

And I still wish it could've been different

But I am no longer afraid, I hold my head high

Each day I live the life I was meant

I know I'm free, forever free

I want the world to know there is life after misery

If I'm weak or strong, if I'm right or wrong

I will not regret, I have left that threat, it's Independence Day

Every day, it's Independence Day


The ring of freedom's bell

Is the only ring I'll ever need

I hear that sound leading me through hell

No matter how much I bleed


I know I'm free, forever free

I want the world to know there is life after misery

If I'm weak or strong, if I'm right or wrong

I will not regret, I have left that threat, it's Independence Day

Every day, it's Independence Day

# In Sleep

That night

I did it

I needed to seal the deal

I won't leave

He won't hurt me

He won't try to take my children from me

The next night

I did it

I figured it was too late to stop now

So I lay

And I took it

But I cried silently afterwards

After that

He tried again

My body shook in rejection

A mixture of disgust and hatred

Churned my stomach

He was scary

And I refused

Last night

I was dreaming

That I was writing a sweet name

On lined paper

And then

Clutching the phone

To my heart

But in sleep

The hard phone

On my warm chest

Became a tough body

On tired flesh

As I awoke

Will I ever sleep again

Am I safe anywhere

How will I ever be free

When can I be myself

# It Scares Me

It scares me

How easy

I know

it would be

to win back my love

so quickly

It scares me

How little

I need

to be happy

It scares me

I don't want to try again

I don't want to die again

I have been slowly dying, alone in my grave

Now I am just beginning

to feel my soul rise again

I don't need to be flesh

a real person

I can be a ghost

a phantom

But if I let myself believe

and go on in this life again

I can't bear to be cut down again


I have just begun to breathe again

I don't want to go back to my coffin and suffocate

# It Would Have

If I had love

I could forgive

a million little sins

I could look the other way

with no anger in my heart

If I had love

I could

let go of anything

I could give up all control

and let life be what it is

If I had love

I could do all the work

and let him play

I would not be tired

I would do anything I could

If I had love

I could please him

many ways

All day and night

With everything I have

It would have been so easy

If he had loved me

# I Used To Think God Cared

I have so many tears

each one cries out

"God do you hear me?

Did You plan this all along?"

My thoughts seep

from first person to third

Did God care about me?

Does He listen to anyone

Why would God test someone like this again; wasn't Job enough?

And I know there is so much more I could suffer; isn't KNOWING enough?

I say time and time again

I don't want to learn any more

Please don't teach me a lesson

Don't I know enough?

Haven't I forgiven

Please don't give me more to forgive

I don't ask how many more times

I need to to give til I can live

# I Wish You'd Believed Me

I wish you'd believed me

when I said

I need some sweetness in my life

please bring me some flowers

sometimes

I wish you'd believed me

when I said

I need the touch of your hand

throughout the day

when you can

I wish you'd believed me

when I said

I need you to hold me when I cry

if I'm not alone

if you're around

I wish you'd believed me

when I said

I need your help through this

every day

if you were willing to

I wish you'd believed me

when I said

if you make me your queen you'll be my king

and I will worship you

constantly

I wish you'd believed me
when I said
I would like to hear some nice words
you don't have to force them
anytime you want

I wish you'd believed me
when I said
I needed a best friend
I wanted to be your soul mate
forever

I wish you'd believed me
when I said
I don't want anyone but you
I gave you everything

and you never accepted it

I wish you'd believed me
when I said
I'm getting tired and worn out
I needed some strength
at that moment

I wish you'd believed me
when I said
I am dying inside
Instead you filled my head
with more promises
I hoped again that you'd keep

I wish you'd believed me
when I said

I can't go on much longer
You asked for another chance
If only you tried to understand
for once

I wish you'd believed me
when I said
I need to be loved constantly
You said you wouldn't give up
it didn't take you long

I wish you'd believed me
when I said
I feel empty inside
You wanted to argue
and I didn't care
anymore

I wish you'd believed me
when I said
I need to see some action
because I don't believe
in your words
in my life

I wish you'd believed me
instead of judging me
I wish you'd believed me
instead of becoming angry with me
I wish you'd believed me
instead of taking it personally
I wish you'd believed me
like a friend

# Knock on the Door

Three times

coming through my door

In one evening,

one night,

Three times,

I can't take anymore

No hoping

No fight

The apology

The bitterness

The drama on the floor

It's too late for me

to feign happiness

I can't take anymore


Flowers do not

make everything better

Their scent does not erase

The stench of hurtful love

What have I got

No love letter

I cannot face

A make believe love


I cried out to God

Please forgive me!

Sobbing til I couldn't breathe

Begging God

Please forgive me!

I don't want to be married anymore.

I don't want to be married anymore.

# Listening

Stillness in the air

Dashes of nature

Birds Calling

Wind

Far off

Very faintly

Drumming

The call to battle

A welcome war

# Lost

Fragmented, broken, lost

I used to have it

A shard of hope

# Love and Grief

Love

I need you

Love

I need to grieve first

I need love

But first I need to cry

Out all the tears

To leave room

For the love

I need

So desperately

I am filled with silent tears

Hidden rain in white clouds

Mist in sunny air

Love wait

Until my grief is gone

# Love Cannot Be Freed

If Love came to me tonight

I would have to put up a fight

And ask "Where have you been"

I've been dragged in

Dove into sin

Now Love can't be right

I don't believe in love

It is a fantasy

Not even from Above

No more bended knee

If somebody wanted me

I could make it so easy

I guess I'd like to need them too

But after all that I've been through

I know it won't be true

No love will ever be


I can't wait anymore

For something that's not real

I have to close that door

In order to feel


I say I don't need love but that is all I need

I say I just want flesh but all I do is bleed

Now there's no way out

Of what this life's about

Nobody hears me shout

I am still waiting to be freed

# Make it Real

I can see my future

And I want it

But if I blink

It could disappear

Like a dream

Fading as quickly

As the nightmare I struggled awake from

Disappears from my consciousness

I want my visions and my hopes,

The heart pounding ideas

To be as real

As the pain and conflict and misery once was

Make it real, keep it real,

Live it for real

# Memorial Day for my Pack

A year ago

He finally

Killed her

She died

With one final swipe

Of intolerance

Of fury

Of hatred

Of Bitterness

Of lust

Lust of control

Rise up girl
Rise up woman
Arise
Live

Little girl
Live again

Live again
Live once
Once more

New life
With the death
Brought on
By
Lack of self control

No

Woman

Down no more


She lives

I live

My girl will remember in her heart

She will know

She will remember

I see it in her eyes

She knows the pain

And that pains me

But never

No more

Never again

She knows that too

My boy

He knows

He's seen

He's heard

He's been there

He's tried his hand

He has given in to that bitterness

That taste unendingly strangling

Now look

His touch is sweetness

His words

Are his own

He says what he feels

He is learning

To speak the truth

In love

A year ago

Living in the turmoil

Of crisis

A year ago

I remember

I remember

I remember


I am alive

Jesus already saved me

I was killed

Now I live again in a new way

I never knew before

My soul was saved

But now my body and heart

Who saved it

Who saved me
Who
Who I love

My children are delivered
From life
Of glass
From moments
Of blindness
From days
Of silence
Of darkness
Of pain
Of lies
They have grieved, they have suffered,
And Jesus,
They are saved

They are saved from this world

Saved from that hand

We will get hurt again

We will feel pain

That is the inevitable fate of life

But Never

Will we be

Under someone else's hand

Never

Will we

Be

At someone else's mercy

Without the ability

To fight back

We can protect ourselves now

We know how to be safe

We are strong

Through our tears

We can still walk

We can still laugh

We can still sing

We can still joke

We can still swim

We can still dance

We can sleep

And we can dream

Together

# Mind Reader

Sometimes it is a good thing

That people don't know what I'm thinking

Because then they would know

How heavily my soul depends on words

How easy it would be to break me down

Or build me up

How quickly I could fall

How tightly I could grasp

How loudly I could scream

How softly I could moan

A song, dancing, in someone's arms

Could throw me into a different universe

Without air or gravity

At times, I feel as if my body needs neither,

    no breath, no structure,

    only a touch, only a whisper

# My Own Betrayal

Humiliation

Tears streaming out of the corners

Of both of my eyes

Sliding onto the pillow

After my body betrays me

To the faceless person

I give myself to

# My Story

My story

Is not just my story

It is my children's story too

For them

I claim anonymity

I do not reveal all

I keep quiet

I compromise

I do not seek validation

I keep the truth to myself

I know

God knows

Eventually

The children will know

More than I want them to know

I will be here

I will acknowledge them

I will answer their questions

With gentleness

Still, always,

It will remain my story

Only God knows

# No One

A handsome guy opened my door today

In that sweet Southern way

He said to me as I walked through

I have something to ask you

Don't you ever get lonely

In the middle of the night

With you and you only

Until the morning light

No one there to hold you

No one there to guard you

No one there to keep you

From monsters out of sight

I patted down my hair from the wind blown wild

As I turned to him and smiled

I said to him as I walked through

I have something to tell you

No one keeps me up all night

When I am trying to sleep

No one hurts me with cruel words

To stab my heart so deep

No one tells me which dreams to hurl

And which plans to keep

I'd rather have no one

Than have some one

When I wake up to a new day

Next to where my little daughter lay

I stretch in my bed and pray

And this is what I say

Thank You God

For no one

No one keeps me up all night

When I am trying to sleep

No one hurts me with cruel words

To stab my heart so deep

No one tells me which dreams to hurl

And which plans to keep

I'd rather have no one

Than have some one

# No Reign

The queen abdicates her throne

Burns her castle to the ground

The dragon devours the kingdom

As she flees

With the prince and princess

Away from this eerie fairytale

With no other ending possible

If she is to lose her vanity

But keep her sanity

# New Year's

What do I have to bring to the table?

Two hands to butter bread.

I used to have more

But now it is all dead.

However, there is still the future

So for this, more wine I pour.

# New Year's Sky

Sparkling tar

Like stars in Abraham's sky

Shining like jewels

Which burst forth from her thighs

Constellations meeting

In an old soul's imagination

Gleaming almost forever

A new year's greeting

# Not Scared

I'm a little scared of how calm I am

Didn't I just lose my man

Shouldn't I be crying now

Shouldn't I be wondering how

I am gonna go on without him

How love could grow so dim

How a spark could die so easily

How I'm okay just to let it be

Why I'm not afraid

I just don't know

What happened to the life we made

It died so slow

But if that's how it's gonna be

I can live with me

# Numb

I sit here on the bench

Like a Catholic school girl early for Mass

So proper and poised

My soul cleansed for the Eucharist

I am out of tears today

My grief has been washed away by the sobbing of agony

In my chest my heart somehow still beats

But I don't feel it

I could forget to breathe

As the numbness of tired pain

Seeps into every cell of my body

What else do I have left to take

What sacrifice must I make

These questions enter my mind

But I don't dare contemplate them

And test fate

# Over

It's okay when it hurts
I don't mind the pain
Because I know it means
It's almost over

When the ripping and tearing begins
I squeeze my eyes shut and relax
It's almost over now
Just wait

With a final burst of pain
I roll over in the night

and sweep my hair over my face

and let the relieved tears drip down

It's over

# Part of Me

Part of me wishes things could be good
and wants to make everything alright
to just run over and say sorry
for everything in the past
for anything I have ever said or done

Part of me cries out
to take another chance
to continue what we have
and see if it could improve

Part of me is sadly glad
a strange mixture
of relief

and pain

and ambivalence


Part of me wonders

what am I going to do

where am I going to go

how will I go on


Part of me wonders

if any of it even matters

# Past and Future

I want the past

    but if I live there

    I'll be a ghost

If I want to live

    I need to move forward

    to a different future

    that is new

# Photos

I live in the pictures

that you can't see

Invisible voyeurs

Reaching for me

Looking out from the colors

Always blindly

Love in poverty

All views are free

# Please

Someday, if I live long enough, if I surpass this, I will write a book...

And I will thank all the people who have helped me...

You don't know what you have done for me, you really don't.

And if I die before then...

Please someday tell my children, I am so sorry...

I am so extremely sorry I let it go on so long and so far.

Please someday, I want to be able to tell them I won for them...

I want them to know what I didn't know.

I want them to be free.

Even if I can never be, please God, let my children be free!

# Please God

Please God

Just listen to me God

I'll tell you how it is God

Just do what I say God

# Pretend

You will see me

And I will smile

And you will look into my eyes

And I will stare with no tears

You will never know

How broken I am inside

How ashamed

How trapped

You won't know

that I am weak

and that my strength

is a sham that shames me

You won't know

All the things taken away from me

And threatened

And feared

You won't know

How out of fright

I have lost so much

And will never regain

I will laugh

I will brush things aside

I will make excuses

And you might believe me

You will see me

Rebuilding what I had
Working with patience
And optimism

You will never notice
How my lips quiver
How my chest tightens
How my eyes squint

I will never let you see
The pain I can't escape

Maybe someday
I will find a way
to live my life
without being held down or held back

Maybe if I work hard enough

If I try hard enough

If I smile enough

If I pretend enough

Maybe in the summer

Maybe in a few years

Maybe in a decade

Or maybe longer

Someday

You will see

After I succeed

# Providing Water

Providing water
Extinguishing flames
That have not yet arisen

# Quiet Burn

Sometimes I burn with anger

But very rarely

More often I ignore what's passed

And face reality

Only if I let them in

Will the images invade

If they have no chance to begin

Then my trembling heart is saved


It's not that I don't thirst for justice

And I'm not trying to make believe

It's just that the heartfelt moments I'd miss

Are worth to much to chance to leave

So in a quiet corner

Only one moment each day

When my mind feels the stir

Of a sad child at play


As sunshine bounces past my eyes

In a darkened room I lay

With clenched fists and tightened thighs

Deeply, for a moment, for this reason, I pray

# Room Mates

Midnight has a way

of figuring out the day

I think I know what it is I want

It makes me laugh

I can feel my teeth

meet each other

in that sardonic way

If I was Billy Idol

you'd know what I mean

I think I want

a

room mate

I don't care

if it's

a

girl

or

a

guy

We don't have to be best friends

or

even

like each other

very much

But I could cook your meals

Not breakfast

Screw that

Only on Sundays

but even the social worker

said I make good coffee

I can't help myself

I want to do that for everyone

and it does make my heart happy

I would do my room mate's laundry

If they wanted me to

But I don't iron

Screw that

I don't even own an iron

I say that with pride

I have never done that

Something I don't do

No patience, why bother

I wouldn't pack a lunch for my room mate

but I would have easy meals

to take along

in the fridge

Dinner

Supper

The big meal

I have that covered

But

You have to understand

What dinner is to me

It is

a grain (carb, like pasta, rice, bread, )

a dairy (milk, cheese)

a protein (cheese, chicken, fish, meat)

2 vegetables or 1 veg 1 fruit (potatoes, green beans, carrots, pears, apples, corn, peas, spinach, marinara)

Sometimes it is pretty

Sometimes it is a jumble

Nothing is wasted

It becomes

Stir Fry

or

Soup

You will be healthy

and satisfied

and if not,

there is always more


I will not ask anything of you

but you are always welcome to join me

on my walks

on my singing

on my dancing

but I would want you to laugh at me and with me

If you can't do that, you can just go to your room and read or whatever

I could entertain you

all night


When you want to move out

you don't need to tell me why

I will be happy for you

that you have different opportunities in life

But if you let me hug you

If you let me kiss you

If you let me hold you close,

then please breathe on me

one more time

And I

will pack

a snack for you

and give you books to read

along the way

# Ruined Makeup

    Leave me alone in my grief

    Sun, shine somewhere else today

    Your warmth only reminds me how cold I am

    Music, stop playing

    Your melody scratches against my heart


    Please don't smile at me

    It makes me wonder why I was denied peace for so long

    When all I wanted was a little kindness


    Now nothing will be enough

    My tears have the courtesy of hiding until I am out of sight

From the world which taunts me

With every bird that flies, every cloud floating in the sky

If only I could really stop believing

If I could give up on hope

My spirit could be calm

# Scanner

This morning I turned the computer on, and it started printing.

It was a photocopy of a page from a notebook I keep in my pocketbook.

    the number of a counsellor at a woman's shelter

    the number and address of a lawyer

    the PD with the name of an officer who was trying to help me

    my sister's cell phone number

    3 websites with divorce advice

Is this what he did when I got the kids ready for their bath last night?

When I was lying down for 10 minutes last night with stomach cramps?

This morning when I drove the kids to school and left my pocketbook at home?

He has ALWAYS needed my help with the scanner, no matter how many times I have shown him, he could never do it himself.

Until now.

The lockbox where we keep all our important information is gone from where it usually is, and the key is gone too.

Yesterday he was very upset when he found a bank slip from an account I opened.

I told him, truthfully, that money is gone now.

This morning he left a "nice" note for me.

I never know how he is going to react to me,

if he is going to be angry for some imagined indiscretion,

or if he is going to completely ignore me,

or if he is going to try to joke with me...

I never know what is going on,

what I am going to get.


Every morning, I awake, not knowing who is waking up with me.

# Shadow of the Cross

I stand by the cross
and feel its shadow on me
the cross which I bear
and I drive into the ground

I look down at my hands
and see no holes in them
I can carry my cross
without being nailed to it

# Shut Up

Silence always kills me

I can bear loud

I can persist in quiet

But stillness, nothingness

Is unbearable

As I slip out beyond the darkness

Preparing to wince against the sun

# Smiling

Smiling

As the key

Opens the PO Box

Smiling

As the check

Deposits in the account

Smiling

As papers

Hide in the locked vault

Smiling

As the doctor

Prescribes birth control

Smiling

As the credit cards

Undergo a name change

Smiling

As the answering machine

Plays messages from men

Smiling

As the taxes

Are filed separately

Smiling

As an honest person

Becomes a villain

# Someone

I want someone to sing me a love song
Bring me flowers tonight
Hold me in warm arms
Tell me everything's all right

Show me the stars
And light up my eyes
Ask me to make a wish
Watch the sun rise

Hold my hand
Take me away
Relax and talk and dream
All night into the day

Feel the rain pouring on us
But it's just fine
Nothing else matters
Just for now you are mine

Brush my hair softly
Feel your fingers on my skin
Dance with me in secret
As sunlight shines in

Look at me and wink
Flash me a smile
Make me feel happy
For just a little while

# Sometimes Rarely Briefly

Sometimes

Rarely

Briefly

I succumb

To

Aloneness

Whimper

Two tears

"I have nobody"

Echos in my ears

But then I come here

I see you

I feel you

All you do

Your

Words

Thoughts

Deeds which I have never thanked you for

The pain turns away

Thankfulness evolves me

My heart strengthens

As I smile

And thank God for you

# Stealth

The warrior is still
and quiet
Stealthily
she performs her tasks
in the camp
which is no longer hers
but is now controlled by
a warlord
Shackles on her wrists
remind her
of what freedom could be
Slowly she sharpens her axe
as if she were in no hurry
but she is biding her time

gaining her strength

aligning her forces

for the day

the drum pounds

and the trumpet

blares her battle cry

# Stigmata

I will close my eyes

I am already nailed to this cross

I asked for this

when I thought it was a tree

A living thing

to plant and grow

But now it is dead wood

heavy and splintered

dry for my blood

# Still

Reading my own words

stuns my heart

so I will just sit here and type

and not look

so my lips won't tremble

and my eyes will not blur

with angry tears

Outside the window

the birds sit

my amusement

my escape

they don't know

they have no idea

And God takes care of the birds!

And He gives them what they need!

Maybe I need too much

Maybe it was better when I was poor and hungry

and didn't think of life

didn't dwell on love

maybe took it for granted

didn't care about doing the right thing

only what I could do each day

to make it through the day


But one day at a time doesn't work for me

I don't have that kind of patience

My heartbeat is an exploding bass drum

My nerves are electric guitars

The calm, quiet peace in my body is fleeting,

I have to invite it in

In my soundless home

I blare the music

that matches my breath

I scream

and I cry

and I kick

and I bang my fists against the windowed doors

I need to have a temper tantrum

There is no alcohol left

What can I do

to get my feelings out?

Who would even listen?
God knows,
but I don't like telling Him
anymore
I am afraid of what He'll say

So many times,
I know God winks at me
or smiles and just shakes His head
at the things I say and do
But this time
He may be talking to me
and I might not want to hear it
So I commit my worst sin
I don't listen

But I'm still here!

Even if I'm invisible!

Even when I'm ignored

and the silence stabs me in the back

until it gouges out my heart

I'm still here

even if

nobody else knows

even if

nobody wants to know

# Supposed

    I was supposed to be the one with a happy home

    The one with the big back yard where all the children roam

    And a big white fence around it, keeping the love safe

    How am I supposed to do this if I am alone


    I was supposed to be the one with dinner on the stove

    The one smiling happy serving meals to whomever showed

    And pretty dishes on the table and flowers in the vase

How am I supposed to do this if I am alone

tell me

tell me


I was supposed to be the one with the diamond ring

The one clapping when sweet children sing

And a Bible in my hand reciting every prayer

How am I supposed to do this with noone else with me


I was supposed to be the one with all that love can bring

The one who could find happiness in almost anything

And willing to do anything to go anywhere

How am I supposed to do this with no one else with me

# Surrender

I put my hands up in the air
And raise my arms to the sky
I quiet the whispers in my ear
And stop asking myself why
I lift my eyes
Tilt back my head and hair
And disbelieve the lies

I surrender
I give up
Lord every time I do
I surrender
I give up
I give myself to You

I believe in God
So I believe in love
I believe in love
Thank You God

I surrender to
The chance of
What could be
What You could do
With love
I give up to be free

# Thank You For Killing Me

What I have to say might sound weird

one of those things that's strange but true

There are many things I have to thank you for

Thank you for killing me so my life could be new


Thank you for all the times you accused me of

cheating lying flirting looking

it was never true, it never happened

My fearful blindness kept my eyes

hidden from the eyes that could have been staring back at me

Thank you for keeping me from vanity

Thank you for letting me believe I was ugly

Thank you for your anger at things I never was guilty of

Now when people compliment me

It means so much more to me

Than all the misery did

Thank you for ignoring me

for hours days and weeks

The anxiety and scorn

that was my every waking moment

drilled into my bones

and now the holes in my being

can be filled

with healing that I didn't know existed

making me stronger

than you ever wanted me to be


Thank you for not being a provider for me and the children

The brief times you did work and bring an income

Were a treat

I never imagined the thought of being upset by your lack of work

Even when I worked two or three jobs and took care of the house and children full time

Even as I built my own business

I will never rely on anyone else

I will never need money from a man

That was never part of my nature to begin with

And you made it easy to never give up my work ethic

Thank you for ruining what I created

My work was the pride of my heart

I was successful, and enjoyed being well known

in the small professional community I started to become part of

Even when we moved, I immediately built it up again

And those new faces joined the family of my heart

My loneliness was eased and my ideas flowed

Oh God how I loved being with those kids

My sweet children loved it too, they learned

so much from sharing their home and lives that way

But thank you

for destroying it

for trying to murder my reputation

Because try as you might

You couldn't get everyone in the world to stop trusting me

And taking my income away

Taking my passion for work away

Gave me less to fight for

and more time to plan my escape

which didn't happen the way I'd hoped

But having less to lose made leaving easier


Thank you for your lies

Thank you for the false accusations

In my bleak desperation I can finally prove

that at least a few of them aren't true

And you prove for everyone to see

how malicious you can be

So I don't have to try to defend myself to you anymore

The begging and pleading, all those times, the

echoes of my agonized voice sickens me

Now every time you attempt to cloud me in doubt

you enshroud yourself in a banner of lies everyone can read


Thank you for standing your children up

and not going to visitation

Honestly, Baby Girl didn't want to see you anyway

Thank you for the way you continue to ignore her

And for how you confuse my Angel

It is the only thing that stirs the anger in me

When they are hurt in any way

When you hurt them, I rise up inside

and feel a surge of powerful protection I never had for myself

And it silently reinforces in their sweet minds

how much better off they are without you

So I don't even have to say one negative word

I never do

I don't have to

You have done it all yourself

So thank you

Thank you for killing me

Thank you for taking everything away

Everything inside my heart has been crushed by you

My soul doesn't know what world it has been in

My mind has been filled with false beliefs

As day by day you cut down the girl I was

Now she is dead

And I thank you

Because now,

She can rise again

And will never be so blind, will never listen, will never

allow anyone to touch her like that

You killed her

and I thank you

Because now

this broken hearted, tired out,

unhopeful woman

has only one thing left to fight for

And I know you must realize this

You promised, you threatened

and I know it's true

that you will do everything you can

to make my life a living hell

and do everything

to take the children from me

because they are

the only part of the last 15 years

which are wholly good

and beautiful

and all I live for

Thank you

for taking away

the distractions of life

which I would have tried to keep intact

Now I have nothing to cloud my vision

Nothing standing in my way

Nothing to cling to or hope for

Nothing to work with

Nothing to fear

All I feared

all this time

was you

Thank you

Now I can be strong enough

even when I cry

to overcome the burden of you

Now I can be powerful enough

even when I don't think God listens

to protect my children, forever

# That's Not

Angry jealousy

Accusing lies

Seething sarcasm

Avoiding eyes

Groping and probing in the night

That's not the kind of love I want

# The Call

She leaned over

The rocky cliff

Bordering the sea

Listening for

The echoing rift

"Love's not calling me"

# Then I Remembered

I almost wished

that he'd grab me

and grasp my stiff arms in his hands

and stare directly into my eyes

and tell me

all the words

I almost wanted to hear

# The Killer Question

The thing that kills me now

is the idea

is the question

I was asked

How would I feel

What would I think of

My SON treating a woman like this

How would I feel

What would I think of

My DAUGHTER having a man treat her like this

Those are the questions

when it comes to my pride

When I know I could give in

When I know I could go on

I would NEVER allow that

I could NEVER put up with that

I would do all my best to set things straight

I would grab my son

by the shoulders

and look straight in his eyes

and tell him

you treat a woman

With LOVE

With COURTESY

With RESPECT

With TENDERNESS

As I type this, I know

He will never be like that

He already knows

Because he treats me

like that

I would grab my daughter

by the shoulders

and look straight in her eyes

and tell her

a man should treat a woman

With LOVE

With COURTESY

With RESPECT

With TENDERNESS

As I type this, I wonder

If she will ever understand that

She is already strong-willed

But I don't know if she would

live like that

For myself,

Yes I know,

I have needs,

all I want and desire

everything I want

could come down to simple words

"love"

"friendship"

I don't need it all

And I don't even WANT it all

# The Song I Sing

This is the song I sing

When no one else is around

And I am wrapped in a blanket

As I wander through the rooms

Inspecting the work

Of my day

Someday

I will be free

Someday

I will be free

Someday

I will be

Free

Someday

My nerves won't tense

When I hear a car approach

Someday

My blood won't burn

When I hear the phone

Someday

I will not hide

Covered in darkness

Of night

Which feels too long

Someday

I will go to bed

And not wonder

If I can sleep

Someday

I won't peer out the corners

of windows

Hoping to be alone

Someday

I will

not be afraid

I will be

who I used to be

Someday

I will be free

Someday

Someday

I don't know when

But someday

I will be free

I sing over and over again

# The Trick

Smiling

As he kisses my cheek

My joy

Is not in love

But in the knowledge

That every day

I get stronger

While he thinks I am weakening


Clenching

My fist at my side

My joy

Is not in love

But in the knowledge

That someday

I will crush him

And take him by surprise

Shocking

My own mind

My joy

Is not in love

But in the knowledge

That evil can

Work for good

That is my choice

# This Is

This is not about now
This is not about then
This is about forever

This
is about
how I always feel
like I need to defend myself
against your accusations
even though I am innocent
and I am sorry
for ever hurting you

This

is about

how I am lonely

when I am with you

even though

I thought we'd always be friends

and I wish we

could have been

This

is about

the way your words change

from nice to sneering

in seconds

and I never know

what is going to happen next

and I am afraid

I will never know

This

is about

how much I have needed

sweetness in my life

just to lift my heart

even though

I am not a pink and purple girl

I cried out so many times

and felt ignored


This

is about

how I wonder why

you never tried as hard

as I think I did

I never needed pretty things

but when you saw me working hard,
did you not care enough
to work hard too?

This is about
years of promises
years of hopes
years of dreams
now I am too old
now I am too tired
now I have told you so much
to make you understand
I wish you'd believed me

# This Morning

This morning he went through my pocketbook and found a notebook.

He flipped through the pages until he found two poems I wrote.

Then he started accusing me of all kinds of things before telling me he read what I wrote.

He didn't listen to what I was saying, he just kept accusing me.


Within an hour he went from accusing me of having obsessions with people,

to being addicted to the internet...

To saying he is done,

he is still young and has his life ahead of him,

and doesn't want mind games...

To telling me that he would call the police and that they would be ready to hunt me down if I ever tried to take the kids...

To saying that I need serious help...

To putting his hands on my shoulders and saying he loves me,

and then pulling me onto his lap and telling me he has hope for us...

This is my morning, this is my day, this is my marriage.

# Thoughts in a Moment

I am like the smoke

From the fire you can't see

I am like the song

From the bird who's never free

I am like the the rain

Soaked into a black cloud

I am like the pain

Kept in a heart too proud

I am searching for a way out

Gasping for life

Like the Earth that spins about

With no end in sight

I am the thudding of a door

In the middle of the night

The creaking of a wood floor

That wasn't set in right

I am the flicker of a candle

You forgot to blow out

I am the dust on the mantle

Being swept about


The star in the sky

That's already burnt away

The breath of a sigh

When you don't know what to say


Dig that shovel in the ground

I don't want to be around

Knowing that the end is near

Leaves nothing less to fear

# Tired of Drama

Last night he told me

I am captivating

that I draw people in

and they are fascinated by me

And when he said that he looked at me

and in my soul I cried

If that is true

If there is something interesting about me

Then why does he barely look at me

How can I mean so little to him

When he got the knife out

he brought it to his chest

and said "kill me kill me kill me"

I was tired of the drama

I wasn't too afraid for him

I wondered if he was serious

But more than that

I was frustrated that he could dare

to act like that

Did he really think I'd drive the knife through his heart

Did he want me to beg plead and cry

I am too tired to have compassion

I wish I cared, but my caring has been used up


Later as I lay in bed with my daughter

In the darkness, I thought about the knife

And how I had threatened to call 911

If he didn't put the knife away

And I thought through the scenario

What if he really does kill himself

I will never be able to forgive myself

His blood will be on my hands

And how sad for my children, for their father to do that

How could I explain that to them


All the tears I cry alone

Because no one wants to hear

All the times my heart breaks

Because nobody really cares


Did I ever ask too much

Did I ever expect more than was reasonable

I know I have been immature

And I have grown a lot through the years

I know I can be many things

Obnoxious when I think I'm funny

Flirty when I think I'm friendly

Trashed when I think I'm having a good time

Melodramatic when I think I'm being deep

Bossy when I am trying to find control

And needy, how I need just a little love

# Today

Yesterday, he wouldn't look at me.

When I tried to make friendly conversation,

he ignored me or barely said uh huh.

I have been setting the table so we sit across from each other,

and he still can't look me in the eyes for longer than 2 seconds.

Last night,

I got into bed,

and he came into bed.

And I was yawning.

And then, at 10:30 PM,

is when he decided to talk to me.

He asked if I want to look at photo albums;

he and Vincent had looked at some the night before.

(hmm, so THAT'S why Vincent was exhausted when he came home from school and crashed into bed,

sound asleep for hours.

And one day last week the poor kid fell asleep in school after another night up with him).

Lots of cute baby pictures and pictures from when Vincent was little.

And he glanced sideways at me and put his hand on mine and said, "We made them."

Which would have been beautiful,

utterly romantic and sweet.

But in my head I was screaming

"NO! God made them!"
Because it revolts me to think of his body with mine.

And he was done looking at pictures,
    and I rolled over to read my book.

Then he lay down,
    covered his eyes.
      And I was yawning.

And at 11:00 he decided he wanted to TALK.

Everything he said had an undertone.
    That is not being paranoid,
    it is the truth.

# Tonight I Sleep

    I don't have to wear layers of clothes tonight

    I won't be stripped while I sleep

    I don't have to sit quietly and wait

    I won't be surprised by who comes to bed with me

    I can read

    I can talk on the phone

    I can cuddle with the kids

    Without interruption

    Without snide remarks

    Without being told not to

Tonight

The only things that will wake me

Are thunder, sleep-talking children,

and the calm dawn

of a new day

    Without prodding and pushing at my body

    Without confusing, hurtful, terrifying words dug into my mind

    Without the constant breaking of my heart

# Wait One More Day

Darkness in the humming air

Delving into deep despair

No hope shines in the starless sky

No use to life, just death, don't cry

Wait one more day

The sun will rise

Beyond the sight

Of cloudy eyes

Wait one more day

Endure, despise

Love will enlight

Through mournful sighs

# Walking Which Way

I thought Jesus would save me

And yes He has saved my soul

Forever

Eternal

My soul belongs to Him

But I thought that

it also meant

He might lift me up

He might whisper to me

and show me the way

But then I stopped LISTENING

because I don't want to hear

that doing the right thing

will cause me a lifetime of pain

Forgive me Jesus

I want to be Yours

but I can hardly bear

this life anymore

I don't want to

start up this marriage again

I really don't want to

let this be how my struggle ends

So Jesus,

How can I do this?

How am I supposed to walk away from my heart

and follow the rules

when I almost feel nothing

# Wanted

I wanted to be married

I wanted to be a good wife

I wanted to have a best friend

I wanted to make coffee every morning and dinner every night

I wanted family portraits

I wanted a happy home

I wanted...


Now part of me is glad the pain is over

The way he'd walk right by me without looking at me

No more sarcasm and mean comments when I am dying for a kind word

# War

An eagle

with talons

Vengeance

Power

I think I liked God better

when He was strong

and would fight

Send Your army God

March Your battalion into my life

If I could raise my sword for You

I would

Cut down in battle

Weaponless

Bleeding

How can I continue the fight

Where is my King

Am I meant to crawl back to the tent

Without victory?

Outfit me, God

with new armor

Tie Your heavy shield to my arm

So I will never drop it

I will lift my sabre again

I will build a new fortress

If only God will

allow it

I will charge

But first I must drag

in the dirt

in my blood

# Warning

Living with nothing

Would suit me just fine

Don't think I am nothing

With what you can't define

I could leave it all

anything

in a heartbeat

in a moment

not a second

I am not yours

I am mine

I live for no one's endeavors

not yours not mine

I will never be owned

I say I own myself

but still remain free

I am owned by no one

not even me

# What

What changed this year
What changed this
What changed
What

# What Pictures

I would tear those pictures up

Drag a black line over them

Sniff my sharpies

and go to town

Nothing would be left of them!

What pictures would I post?

Which photographs

would have meaning?

The wedding

that's THE day

The day

that began and ended

all other days

Would I post

the pictures in our apartment

I was so thin tan and sexy

and hungry and poor and needy

But still I was strong

I never gave up

Would I post

the pictures by the ocean

with hopes and dreams

with ideas of the future

that would never appear

Would I post

the pictures after I prayed

and God told me to trust Him

and I still believe Him!

Would I post
the pictures of our house
of our baby boy
my tired Christmases

Would I post
the pictures of me all night
with my children
exhausted like no one else

One day I came home
between shifts
and the children fell asleep
And I collapsed on the bed
even though I still had so much work to do

And in my blurried thoughts I remember

thinking, I hope there's not a fire

because I don't know if I'd be strong enough

to save us all!

Would I post

the pictures before we moved

the house filled with children

Some of my happiest days!

Now those pictures make me cry

those children I no longer KNOW!

Those babies I watched grow

will never know me again

Would I post a picture of our new home

our new dreams

our new thoughts

our new hopes

When did I have my last dream

When did I stop believing?

Was it when I was all alone

To do EVERYTHING?!

# What is Wrong With Me

For fifteen years I was a good wife.

I cooked,

I cleaned,

I worked,

I took care of the children.

I was entertaining,

I was funny,

I was thoughtful,

I was kind,

I was caring,

I was patient,

 I was helpful,

I was attentive.

I didn't nag,

I didn't complain,

I didn't bitch,

I didn't judge.

So what the heck is wrong with me?

Why is it so hard to love me?

Why was it so hard to be nice to me?

All I wanted,

    was a tiny bit of kindness.

    I would have been so satisfied.

Why did I get misery and anger and grief?

Constant anguish,

and I still hoped,

I still tried,

I still did my best and gave my all.

Is it so hard to just be nice to me?

What is wrong with me?

# What Is It To Me

To me

it is a vague memory

quick blurred snapshots

overexposed

It is a dead thing

with air blowing over it

making it appear alive

It is a broken dream

with no happy ending

because the night is over

It is a vacuum of space

suffocating

taking air from life

It is unreachable

untouchable

unreal

It is make believe

internal lies

false

And

it courses through me

beyond me

without my control

strong in its own power

but I will never hold it

I will never touch it

it's not for me to have

# When

When I

was just a girl

I wondered

if God

just wanted me for Himself

if there was no one else

who could fill my void

who could match me in this world

and I wanted to serve Him

When I

was a young mother

the priest asked me

to say

what I would like to say
to Jesus right now

and I said

I will listen to You, Jesus

And throughout the years
I have listened
and I have heard
and I have not ignored
And I have knelt down
and obeyed
and I have been tried and tested
And I never gave a second thought
to my vow
of listening

But now

I feel like it's been so long

And I still love my Lord

but doesn't He want me to have love?

I would want it for myself

if I was Him.

If I was Him

I would have stopped me

long ago

And maybe it's true

that I have learned a lot

I thank God from the bottom of my heart

for my suffering

I know hunger and poverty

I have looked it in the eye

I have been there and tasted it

I do not judge

I do not ask

to be rewarded for my pain

but maybe

God could be merciful in this?

Could he give to this spoiled child

what her heart desires

even if it is not in the written plan

could it be good anyway?

Oh God,

Don't you hear me?

Don't you see me?

Don't you feel the tears falling down

YOU created me,

YOU gave me this life

Please forgive me God, for blaming you

for the pain I feel in my heart!

But as I cry alone,

who will help me,

who will love me?

You gave me this body

which craves the warmth I want

You gave me this senseless mind

which maybe thinks too much

So if you wanted me, God,

why didn't you take me

before it was too late?

If you had a different plan for me,

why didn't you stop me?

I think I would have heard you
way back then!

I am sorry God.
I am sorry that I feel this
neediness
of a bratty little child
I know you have given me so much
I know you have saved me from so much more!

So please forgive me,
if I would like you to indulge me.
I still want love.

# Which Voice Do I Hear

Will God forgive me

for breaking this vow

Will He still help me

if I do the wrong thing

Will He still

talk to me

Will I still hear Him?

Because I haven't been listening for a while

and that is my sin

I have opened my ears

for the devil to whisper

And I have heard all the words

that I wanted to hear

# Why it is not Good to be Alone in my Thoughts

I just realized,

I am sitting with my feet up on the couch,

and at this moment,

I am not afraid.

I am crying now,

out of relief and grief,

I AM free.

Never again!!!!

Never will he touch me like that,

never will he push me like an invisible animal into the wall,

in his way,

never will I wait and talk and try and search and get nothing but pain with brief flashes of false apologies and my never ending forgiveness and patience and kindness.

Please God,

I pray through my tears,

let me be a bitch,

now that I am away from that heartache,

let me be the tough,

strong woman

I always thought I was.

Let me live with my two sweet children in a home where we can overcome and enjoy life together, let me show them what being a woman means

that tough isn't putting up with abuse;

tough is leaving it.

God, help me, please!

# Words and Voices

In the quiet of my mind

my thoughts speak out loud

And the voice wonders

what I should do

Should I kiss and make up

Should I grovel and plead

It would be worth it

To not have to see

those sad children's faces again


But then my friends say


You are not that kind of person

You're better than that

Don't back down

Don't give in

They say

it's been a long time coming

and I've been more patient than most

don't hurry to him

Don't do it for the kids

they will be alright

They don't know how I've put up with so much already

But their words

are not louder

than the voice in my head

What they say

does not take away

my children's tears

So what do I do?

Do I take drugs and move on with a marriage

that continues to kill me inside

I would rather be dead

than hurt those kids again

I could suck it up, smile,

pretend to forget

and be a family once more

# Written Earlier, True Every Day

Tonight before I end my day

I'll get down on my knees and pray

For all the people in my life

Who have helped me through this gripping strife

In my darkest days

When faith crumbles

Like dry clay

Light shines through

These neighbours, friends, strangers

If only they knew

My hidden dangers

They protect me from

Without even trying to

# Written In Fear, Never Again

Today I cried

Because I knew

That it was true

There's so much he could do

To hurt me

To make me bleed

For my kids to be free

Is what I need

Today I cried

Because I see

He can still hurt me

He could still take from me

If he got the chance

I think he would rape me

# Yesterday

Yesterday

A neighbour came to the door

And she asked if

I was around.

He answered the door

and the children ran over

to see who was there

(I think they miss people coming over)

and he said

I don't know where she is.

My neighbour told him, she just wanted

to see if I wanted to go for a walk with her.

Just then I came down the stairs,

(it was bath time for the kids)

and heard her, and glanced at the little scene,

and quickly said YES, I'll be right there.

I changed my clothes,

and thanked God,

He must have heard me holding in my tears

as I repeated to myself

"Do I exist?"

Before I left, I told the children

I would be back soon,

I was just going for a walk,

and were they okay with that,

and they smiled and said, yeah!

And I asked him,

as he sat, pink faced and tense,

Is it okay that I am going out?

And he turned his head slightly to briefly glance at me

and said

Why wouldn't it be?

In a voice, the tone, his angry eyes...

And I said, I don't know, it's bath time, then bedtime...

And he said

No. Go.

So, I smiled, and did.

I was so grateful to this woman.

I think she is trustworthy.

And when she had a tough time a year or so ago, and

the neighbourhood was full of gossip

I kept my mouth shut

and tried to lift her up when I saw her.

On our walk,

she told me,

she had come to the door before,

that night all hell broke loose,

and he had told her

I wasn't around

I was away

because I was popping pills.

When I came back from the walk,

the kids were just getting out of the bath,

and I helped them get ready for bed

and tucked them in

and cuddled with baby girl.

And I drifted off in her bed

but woke up

and heard my bedroom door close.

I got up, to get ready for bed

and couldn't turn the knob on my bedroom door.

It was locked.

I knocked.

He said

Yes?

And I asked to come in please

and he said okay

and I heard papers rustling and the bed creaking and footsteps

and after about thirty seconds I jiggled the knob

and said

it's locked

and waited

for him to open it

then said

Thanks.

And finally, it was eleven o'clock

the lights were all on

I crawled into bed with my security blanket book

and he decided

he wanted to talk.

Which now I know really means

he wants to ask me questions

that are hard for me to answer

and that he won't be satisfied with

no matter what I say

and instead of talking to me

he uses sarcasm

and disagrees with how I say I feel

and accuses me of twisting HIS words around

and then says he sees this is going to turn into an argument

and turns away.

And he said,

I know you're lonely, and I am sorry you feel that way.

And I smiled and said, no, I'm not lonely.

And he looked surprised,

and I was surprised too, because I realized,

I really am not lonely.

I have FRIENDS.

And he said well,

I know you're sad, and I hate it for you.

(he has never spoken to me with this voice of empathy before, it turns out he had just read a book chapter about empathy)

And I smiled and shook my head and said

no, I'm not sad.

(I do not mope, I smile when he sees me, I know that)

And he looked surprised again.


And he said,

Do you feel desperate?

And a red flag went off in my head, wondering, where is he GETTING this?

And I said NO, not at all.

And I said, I am glad that now he knows, he does NOT know how I feel,

I am my own person with my own feelings

(the book I am reading says to make statements like this)

And I repeated it

And he looked agitated and said he sees where this is going,

I am twisting things into circles.

And I said no, I am telling him how I feel.

And he said, well how DO you feel

(and this whole time his face is pink, and he is sharing NOTHING)

and I smiled and slowly said

Encouraged Empowered Hopeful

And he inhaled, and

looked like his wind had been taken away.

And I asked HIM

if HE was lonely if HE was sad if HE was desperate

and he briefly answered no.

And he asked what I want for the future, for our family,

and I said

happiness.

And he lay down

and was silent

And said it seems like all he is getting from me is

one word answers so he is not going to bother.

And I told him, well, that is my answer, I don't know what answer he was looking for.

And I said, maybe you should answer your own questions,

(I say this lately sometimes)

and he replied, well, I'm not asking him.

So I asked him what does he want from the future

and he said

oh so piously

He follows God and he will go where God leads.

That was my night.

This morning

he brushed by me quickly, almost bumping into me

never looking at me

By the door, he said "excuse me"

and I tried to move out of his way

because I realize now

that when he says excuse me

he doesn't wait

he just pushes through, knocking into me

(he did this yesterday too)

and when I didn't move fast enough

he said

I need to get by.

And I said I am trying to move out of your way.

He didn't give me any room to MOVE.

Then, he comes back from dropping the kids off at school

And asks me

Are you afraid of me?

And I was too afraid to answer him.

And the way he said it, was like a quote, he does that a lot,

so I asked him, with a smile,

Is that from a movie?

And he said no.

And I said oh, it sounded like something Jack Nicholson would say.

Still with a small smile.

And he repeated the question.

But I didn't have an answer.

So after about fifteen seconds he said,

he guesses I am not going to answer.

And of course, all this is from across the room.


Then he says

let's talk

Sure, fine, I felt okay with that.

We sat on the couch

And he asked me questions

And lectured me that actions speak louder than words

and that he is giving to me and that I am not giving anything back

And pointed out that I never call him at work

And that during the day he knows I have at least the mornings free

and wonders how many times I drive by

and never stop in

And do I want to be married anymore,

because he is on the fence

and if this keeps up the way it is

he isn't sure what there is for us


And the whole time

I am smiling

Because

I am thinking

This doesn't hurt anymore

Not because I am ignoring my feelings

but because I honestly don't care what he thinks anymore

And because I know

I have friends

who DO care about ME!

And they think I have a good future ahead of me


And he asked me again

if I am afraid of him

And I avoided it

and he asked more

and I asked

Why would I be afraid of you?

And he didn't really have an answer

And I asked him

what makes you think I am afraid of you

and he said

because I lock the front door

every day

when he takes the kids to school.

He had made a point of telling me

"Actions speak louder than words"

So I asked him if in this case,

my action of locking the door was speaking to him that

I was afraid of him.

And he said it says to him that I don't want him in the house.

And I said, oh so it hurts your feelings, but

it is a safety habit of mine to always lock the front door of the house.

And he replied that no,

it doesn't hurt his feelings anymore, he's used to it.


Then I leaned forward

a smile on my face

and said

Oh, so a locked door to you

is actions speaking louder than words

that I don't want you in the house?

And I drove that point home, smiling, and repeating myself

for clarification, asking him, what does the action of locking a door say to him?

And he stood up and walked away.

I asked

What are you doing?

(just like the book I have been reading says to do)

and he said

getting more coffee.


And he asked me again

am I afraid of him

and I should have just avoided him

but he wore me down, I should've shut up somehow

but I said maybe.

And I swear he smiled a little.

And I asked him

Would it make you happy if I was afraid of you?

And he said no.


And I told him,

how I would like him to understand

after all these years

of me

being alone

working all day

with no phone call from him,

and even when he was unemployed at home

or last year doing real estate and he'd be upstairs

on the laptop looking up Major League Baseball

he didn't come to hang out with me,

we just don't have that kind of relationship,

so of course, after all these years of living like this,

it never even occurred to me

to call him,

because he never did that for me.

And he said

No, he called me, he remembers in construction

calling from a pay phone.

And I didn't let that one slide, now that we were talking about it.

I said,

Very, very rarely.

When I was expecting Vincent, he called a few times,

then he got a pager

then he never called again.

And he didn't deny it.


After pausing for a few minutes,

he said,

he's changing,

he's a different person now.

And he is sorry if my feelings were hurt all those years.

I told him, my feelings weren't hurt, that was normal life for me.

And he asked, That was normal life, and it didn't hurt your feelings?

And I told him, how could it hurt my feelings

when I never knew any other way.

And he said well now, looking back,

does it hurt?

And I said I haven't had a chance to look back yet

but that is just my life, that is my every day, how could it hurt,

it's like saying "Today is Friday"

it doesn't hurt, it is just a fact of life.


There is so much, so much so much

every word

he can't back up

All the insinuations

I just don't have the energy to type

He finally left

after kissing my on the mouth before

I subtly pulled away,

after leaving a note that says

I love you! You are very special.

and when he left I read it and cried

because I can't believe him

Other people, my friends,

I know they care about me

and when they tell me that I am special

even if it is hard for me to comprehend

I let it float in my brain

But when he wrote it,

it seemed false, like a trick

He came back

with six red roses

and a CD

I guess that means everything is great

and he is SO thoughtful and caring

and I should be grateful

He left again

I turn to God and ask

Are you watching?

Do you see this?

# Thank You

Thank you for reading "Freedom for Me," my collection of poetry about surviving domestic abuse and violence. As an independent author, I rely on book reviews to spread my message and to reach new readers. Please take two minutes to rate and review "Freedom for Me" on Amazon and Goodreads. Your one sentence review could make a big difference in my readership!

"Freedom for Me" on Amazon: https://www.amazon.com/Jessica-Lucci/e/B075JMNK1S

"Freedom for Me" on Goodreads:https://www.goodreads.com/author/show/17157283.Jessica_Lucci

# Acknowledgements

People supporting each other through space, time, words, and action, is magic.

I have experienced this magic. I hope this book can spread a flicker of freedom, hope, strength, solidarity, courage, and awareness to all people enduring domestic abuse and violence.

With thanks to all the angels in human form who walked with me through my personal hells.

The doctor who didn't charge me for the appointment when I begged for an IUD so I wouldn't get pregnant by my husband's rapes.

A co-worker who brought in sandwiches every day for her and I to eat together: I never told her how hungry I was.

A relative who out of the blue sent me a check for one hundred dollars; she had no idea that it saved me from losing my electricity again.

My bosses who took me aside and insisted I allow them to bless me by providing school supplies as Christmas gifts to my children.

The anonymous neighbour who dotted my lawn with Easter eggs for my children to wake up to.

My former middle school teacher who reached out to me with words of encouragement and kindness to my children.

The neighbour who drove me to work because my car needed repairs I couldn't afford.

The therapist who didn't pursue payment when her business office realized they had been charging too low of a fee.

The police officer who gently advised me that I should leave my husband because it was not healthy or safe for me and the children to stay with him.

My parents, my siblings, my friends, who all gave their love, support, time, money, patience, and strength as I struggled to free my children and myself from the house of hidden violence.

These, and many more human angels, who in all ways brightened my dark road to freedom. There are not small ways, or big ways, just ways, and I am grateful for you all.

# Resources

The National Domestic Violence Hotline: http://www.thehotline.org

National Coalition Against Domestic Violence: https://ncadv.org/get-help

Jane Doe Inc.: http://www.janedoe.org/find_help

Respond, Inc.: https://www.respondinc.org

Family Violence Prevention Services: https://www.benefits.gov/benefits/benefit-details/626

Patricia Evans, writer of domestic abuse and violence, author page:https://www.amazon.com/Patricia-Evans/e/B001JPCCWY/ref=dp_byline_cont_ebooks_1

# About the Author

Jessica Lucci perseveres in her recovery from abuse and proudly advocates for mental health. She makes her home in Massachusetts, USA.

Free words flow here:
https://www.jessicalucci.org


Facebook: https://www.facebook.com/Jessica-Lucci-1574551225939780/

Twitter: @Jessica__Lucci

Amazon Author Page: https://www.amazon.com/Jessica-Lucci/e/B075JMNK1S

Goodreads: https://www.goodreads.com/author/show/17157283.Jessica_Lucci

YouTube: https://www.youtube.com/channel/UC-5CPSykd5gYM5Abfrt8b-A

Instagram: https://www.instagram.com/jessica__lucci/

LinkedIn: https://www.linkedin.com/in/jessica-lucci-315045142

Pinterest: https://www.pinterest.com/indiewoods/pins/

Jessica Lucci web page: https://www.jessicalucci.org

# Also by Jessica Lucci

**Justice for the Lemon Trees**

Exhilarating waves of emotion pound on the shores of pages pebbled with tragic child abuse, brash bullying, and calamitous schooling. Ms. Lucci's memoir follows a fierce young girl from suburbia to an engulfing ocean of adult bleakness. Through her eyes, and in her own words, we bear witness to her agonizing submission and defeat in domestic violence, and lift our hearts with hers as she rises up above savage shame. Agonizingly, she falls into despair and uncertain madness as she loses everything, all over again. Through her life story, we can trace the path of pain to follow where things went wrong, and how they can be repaired for the hope of future happiness, for all survivors and their families.

## Person Numbers: Poems from Prison

This collection of poetry written by an inmate in a women's correctional facility imparts the range of pain, loss and grief, as well as the flashes of friendship and hope, which exist behind bars.

## Code Words

Exploring physical and emotional feelings while battling mental illness. Pain, desperation, and hope are expressed soulfully in this poetry anthology.

## To Die a Bachelor

Aggie is incarcerated. She can deal with that. But when tragedy strikes she must find a way to empower herself. Joining forces with her orange clothed peers, she builds ingenious schemes, elicits illicit love, and spreads her fire of inspiration.

# Coming Soon
# By Jessica Lucci

## From the Big House

Twelve women, twelve months. Connected by food and time, each woman shares the same dark secret, although each one keeps it differently. As the year progresses into mish-mashed adventures, the haunting truth comes full circle to encompass them all.

## Seasons

New England poetry exploring nature, time, and phases of life.

# Justice for the Lemon Trees

## IHIBRP Recommended Read 5 Star Award Winner

Exhilarating waves of emotion pound on the shores of pages pebbled with tragic child abuse, brash bullying, and calamitous schooling. Ms. Lucci's memoir follows a fierce young girl from suburbia to an engulfing ocean of adult bleakness. Through her eyes, and in her own words, we bear witness to her agonizing submission and defeat in domestic violence, and lift our hearts with hers as she rises up above savage shame. Agonizingly, she falls into despair and uncertain madness as she loses everything, all over again. Through her life story, we can trace the path of pain to follow where things went wrong, and how they can be repaired for the hope of future happiness, for all survivors and their families.

https://www.amazon.com/Justice-Lemon-Trees-Jessica-Lucci/dp/0999410040/ref=asap_bc?ie=UTF8

"Justice for the Lemon Trees" is Author Jessica Lucci's personal memoir of "tragic child abuse, brash bullying, and calamitous schooling". Plagued by domestic violence, and an unfair social services system that would rather imprison women than provide the mental healthcare they need and deserve, Lucci rises up time and again through despair, loss, and tragedy to become an effective advocate for others walking the most difficult paths of life, leading them from helpless victim to proud survivor.

For once, I'm not going to expand on the author's writing style—which, by the way, conveys the real-life, nitty-gritty life she has endured. I am only going to say that, for anyone who has experienced childhood sexual-abuse, bullying, domestic trauma, and the misfortune of being completely misunderstood and discounted, meet your kindred soul-survivor. I highly recommend this book to anyone seeking to understand how a person who is broken down time and time again still has the courage and fortitude to rise up and become a beacon to others.

To Author Lucci—for all the life lessons you had to learn the hardest way possible, for all the bright spots you sparked in a sea of misery, for all the work you do to help those survivors of abuse and trauma today—I'll just say a simple, "Thank you for being who you are today."

-Author JB Richards

# Person Numbers

This collection of poetry written by an inmate in a women's correctional facility imparts the range of pain, loss and grief, as well as the flashes of friendship and hope, which exist behind bars.

https://www.amazon.com/Person-Numbers-Prison-Jessica-Lucci/dp/0999410032/ref=asap_bc?ie=UTF8

A combination of poetic expressions that took me inside the author's world. The poems tugged on my emotions with every turned page as I explored the writer's inner thoughts. These gift of poems showed that it doesn't take a whole lot of empty words to speak to truth, a few powerful profound words will get the job done. Well written, Lucci. This is a great comfort read and now that I'm reading the book's companion, Justice for the Lemon

Tree, Person Numbers has taken on new clarity. The two books make for a great gift to you and for someone who's facing tough times.

   -Author Connie Spencer

# Code Words

### Readers' Choice Award Cover of the Month 3rd Place

Exploring physical and emotional feelings while battling mental illness. Pain, desperation, and hope are expressed soulfully in this poetry anthology.

https://www.amazon.com/Code-Words-Jessica-Lucci-ebook/dp/B078HNTLZ2/ref=asap_bc?ie=UTF8

Impressive.

-Author Zev Good

# To Die a Bachelor

**Amazon #1 New Release**

Aggie is incarcerated. She can deal with that. But when tragedy strikes she must find a way to empower herself. Joining forces with her orange clothed peers, she builds ingenious schemes, elicits illicit love, and spreads her fire of inspiration.

https://www.amazon.com/Die-Bachelor-Jessica-Lucci-ebook/dp/B07B9132W2/ref=asap_bc?ie=UTF8

This is a story that seems broken up in episodes rather than a flow of a novel... it is an incredible story of broken people who apparently must've had horrendous lives and you can see how it's the apathy that they feel at times that enables them to do what they did. There is such a tenderness in the midst of this brutality that it just touches one's heart. There's a beautiful story between Angie and Bunkie, and how they support one another in a place where there is little hope. They find ways to amuse them self and stay active. When Angie's son is hospitalized the women who she is friendly with in prison all do their best to find ways to earn money to send to help with his care. While she is powerless to help her son there's such a ray of hope when all the women step up to help her.

    -Amazon Book Reviewer Ro Fetterman

# Your Page

This page is for the reader to write in or rip out as desired. Your words, thoughts, and ideas matter.

www.ingramcontent.com/pod-product-compliance
Lightning Source LLC
Chambersburg PA
CBHW020922090426
42736CB00010B/1006